# POETIVITY

# POETIVITY

**I Will Rise stronger**

No one is beyond remedy. It would be
a tragedy to think otherwise.

## samson yung-abu

Rev. date: 08/18/2021

**To order additional copies of this book, contact:**
Xlibris
UK TFN: 0800 0148620 (Toll Free inside the UK)
UK Local: 02036 956328 (+44 20 3695 6328 from outside the UK)
www.Xlibrispublishing.co.uk
Orders@Xlibrispublishing.co.uk
830336

# Introduction

If you believe that you deserve better, this book is for you. If you believe that you are worth the effort, this book is for you. If you are unsure of what you want in life, this book is for you. Now, are you worth better?

# What is Poetivity all about?

Poetivity is a well-packaged source of positive energy and a great vibe to help create a better life for yourself and those around you. At its core, poetivity speaks from pain, happiness, love, creativity, passion, and experience—evoking change and a drive to reach for the goals you set. Imagine just for a second. Now, where you wanted to be a few years ago; how much better would your life be today? Poetivity is also about taking daily disciplined steps toward a happier future. Why steps? Steps are so critical in life; they are so decisive in each present moment in time. The steps we take or don't take determines how dominant or dormant our sense of value will be in the future. As this collection of powerful positive poems and prose reveals, we must never waste another day without taking a step in the direction we want in life. Anything little will do. Doing nothing at all won't do.

# I Will Rise stronger

No matter how the night sky arrives,
we must want to arise brighter!

# More still Left in Me

There is more still left

with me, more still left
of me. I know what you
see, yes, I am a book with
a battered cover. With
chipped edges. With
missing pages. With

a flawed spine. I am

worn and torn, tough
but flammable, a mess
with much missing.
But what still lies inside of

me are stories with
many happy endings.

# I Rise and Shine

I open my eyes
and rise. Hello gorgeous,
hello handsome, hello
sunshine, the morning

sun greets me in many

shines. I smiled at my
kind. It is time to drive
away my shades and

shadows.
I rise and shine.

# This Ain't No Time to Cry

This ain't no time to cry,

fly strong bird. Backed into
the corner by past mistakes,
barking at me with blames.
Too much pain I feel, and
this pressure is making my
wings feel too weak to try.
But endured I have, for I have
seen many strong winds in
my past. So, this ain't no
time to cry. I can't keep

looking back, there is no

luck going back. I feel the
wind in the sky. I've gotta
test these wings I own. Walk
a few steps I must. Fly my
strong wings I must. Work
onwards I must. For I see the
bright light within me, leading
me through the darkness around me.
There it is. After this many miles,
I can see a sky of rainbows
through this dark tunnel.
What a turn of event my effort
has lead. This ain't no time to
cry, you must fly, strong bird.

I will never stop reminding
myself.

# I Will Rise stronger

I have grown other's happiness like the sky,
helped them bloom like the sun. Water my soul,
drain me from my sadness anew. Is it too much
to ask of myself after all I have done to please
others? No, it's the least I could do for myself!

# I Refuse to Cast Aside My Last Try

I refuse to cast aside my last try, for every crevice of my dream is divine. Even though this scary world has given me many scars, diminished everything I have attempt until I feel finished, until I feel crushed and perished. But still, I will keep going.

I will wear these scars like medals around my neck, let them bounce and shine as I take each courageous step into another height.

For so long, I have let doubt delay my blessings, leaving me in decay. Rotten with dead dreams. But today, I declare my faith with a fight against the version of me I want to change for good.

Change is a choice, an option I have ignored all along, but now I choose to ascend into the version I am destined to become. For mediocrity is not what my mama gave birth to. With boldness, I shall continue to unfold. For within discomfort, I now set to challenge my comfort.

# what's poetry to you?

                    Poetry is my oxygen,
my volition, my prosperity,
my vitality and liberty.
Poetry is my source of energy,
my space of peace,
my power, my poison of choice.
                    Poetry is my emotional freedom,
my seek and find,
my place of nest, to invest what's dearest.
                    Poetry is my perfect pleasure.
                    Poetry is my treasure.

# still I keep Going

Intentions high, ambition high,
action I take. Nothing can take me
down from what I want to make
of me. And even as I went along, I stumbled.
Even as I went along, I tumbled
Even as I went along, I scrambled.

But none of it was strong
enough to crumble my hope.
Even without appreciation,
even with endless distraction around me,
even with endless temptation to quit,

even with endless condemnation,
Still, I keep going.

# what an Asset I Am

All the rejections, all the
abandonment, made me
a better company to myself.

Now I have become the
best asset to my own

happiness.

# I Will Rise stronger

The recipe for your happiness is in
the details of your past!

# If only

If only you were willing to

wipe the tears you created,
you would have seen that
gold covered in dirt never

loses it value. If only you

would have washed my
fears with your love, you
would have seen that my
heart is a priceless art in a

museum of
expensive women.

# My Humble Pen

Like sperms approaching eggs, my thought races to the sharp of my humble pen. Linking the ink to my thinking. Linking my thinking to the tip of my pen. I am not just a writer, but like any man, I am, with many kinks I am, but thinking in ink is my real deal. I am liking this chain of events, but the speed still anchors me to so much doubt. Will I make it? Will I finish this story that I am writing? These flickering thoughts, I am sure we've all had. I am not liking this brink. I smell doubt, but I am not out of believe yet. I know that I am due to win anytime soon, even though this weight in my mind is taking more than nine months to deliver. Any time now will be great.

Through all my previous writing and winnings, I do not forsake that wiring is a patient process to success, barring for quitters, and a wait never means baring to defeat, a wait never means barring to produce, for a wait bears great things. And like a pregnant woman, we must pray on it, we must care for it, we must take care of ourselves so that the self within us can come out better, capable of holding itself among its kind. I will be patient with me, my humble pen.

# I Will Rise stronger

The people that understand us in our silence know the voice that speaks pain. They connect to our soul for life!

# -Oh, Oh, Oh, Mental Health: I Am No Stranger to These Walls, I Know This Fall

As this morning borns, the black dog barks. My eyes crack open, but my feet feel burdened with no desire to see the world. The bell rings for a while for me to get up, but my mood feels not so well. I can tell it's going to be a long, bad day. Oh, oh, oh, mental health: I am no stranger to these walls, I know this fall.

Today, lie and wait is all I can do till I can break out of my depressed cocoon bed, till my walls turn to strong wings. But for today, in this bed, I must float till a bright sky calls, till it's time to fly again. Oh, oh, oh mental health: I am no stranger to these walls, I know this fall.

My bed holds me in solace as last night's peace turns into tears on my face. The seasons have changed without warning, and the warmth is now filled with faults. My flaws fly for fun, I know I am ugly without looking at any mirror. I judge myself so people can be satisfied that I accept what they were trying to tell me. Oh, oh, oh mental health: I am no stranger to these walls, I know this fall.

My dress calls me. My phone pings at me. Everything tries to get me up and going today. But my mind dries of all tries. All I can say is please forgive me, I wish I could do more than try. Please understand me, I wish I could do more than explain. Oh, oh, oh mental health: I am no stranger to these walls, I know this fall.

# HOPE

Everything

smells of strange sorrow.
But the hope

of tomorrow,

it smells of home.

# I Will Rise stronger

If anyone is holding you back, it's because you have let them feel stronger than they are!

# Burden of a Lover

I don't want more.

I just want less of this pain
that I bared so long,
carrying more than my heart,

and yours, carrying

more of your blame
than you do.

I don't want more,
no more.

# It's All in Your Mind

Me: Success, where are you at?

Success: Right here in your mind.

Me: Ooh. Tell me what to do please to succeed?

Success: If you want to succeed, you have to progress.

Me: How do I progress?

Success: You must be fully committed to the process of making your dream happen.

# when someone cares

No one cared when I was broken.
No one cared when I was betrayed.
No one cared when I am hurting.
No one cared when I was starving.
No one cared when I was knocking.

The same happened to my uncle, but now he is gone, bones grinding still in his grave, many shed shady tears. Friends, relatives, or enemies, it is hard to tell from this bunch, crunching tissues without tears. Many among them weren't there when he needed them to be there. Fake hands holding real flowers. He shall be missed they say, missing the part where they never cared.

This tells me the tales of my generation, that no one wanted to hear. The one that everyone fears all too well. No one cares until you become a diamond, and they all want a cut.

Now I know, no one would care until I am gone.

But gone I will be, just not in a grave beneath dust and dirt. Now, I go away from my old self, changed my shame to fame, framed my version in the best mansions, with wheels well spent. With watches with B prices. Now they cared to want to know me. What a shame to know that no one would, when we are long gone, but if you know me when I am down, I shall know you when you are down. Like I have become, you will be. You shall be welcome in my home when I sky high. This is what happens when someone cares when I needed them to be there.

## Through Pain I Shall Move into My Purpose

Each time the sky lets

go of the night, the
sun that usually shines
on earth becomes a ball
of clouds barricading
the sunlight. My palm,
which holds hope like a
lamp, continues to unfold,

directing me as my feet

move through all possible
corners. Like a bush in
flame, burning through
everything in its path

till the path is cleared
for a greater purpose.

# Wind Much High

For a while, a strong bird like
me was pressed against the
inside of a cage. Winds much
higher I would never know.
With mice and snails, life
made me to stay. Unlike this
kind that would never fly,
my fate was tied to two
strong wings. But I was unable

to get going—because

I never knew where I wanted
to go. Dawn came and dusk
waned, and still I am framed
in this cage. But what good
is a strong bird if it can't fly
towards the sky? I asked myself.
Right then, I realise that one
can't get going until one sets
a goal on the go. Right then,
I look at the sky above my
cage. Right there, I made a
goal to get out of my cage.
Right now, I am in the sky
among my kind, in winds

much higher than than I
ever knew.

# I Will Rise stronger

I can't be trapped. I flow like a river. I fly like smoke. I move like the day!

# purpose

Until I find my purpose,
I shall not rest. This was
a promise I vested in my
heart. So in my purpose I

began to invest. And in

my pursuit of prosperity,
I found out that it is not

politics but purpose that
changes poverty.

# A Work in Progress Is All
# I Can Be Right Now

Flaws crawl all over me
at the mirror of my mind
against your mean words.
I cry and cry and cry until
I can fake a smile again.
Perfect! I bark softly as I
smack my lips together, like
a lady with fresh lush lipsticks. Though, due still
remains, for each time nothing
overdue changed, your words
are still mean, and teary
emotions still flood
my mood. Each time
everything remained
constant, like the fake
smile I have mastered
over time. But now I feel
pleased, ignoring your flaw
calls. And now calm I
have claim for a work in

progress is all I can be
right now.

# I Will Rise stronger

You are the reason I keep shining. But, without you watching me, my shining star won't matter!

## Beauty Everywhere, Glamour all Around Me

Beauty everywhere,
glamour all around me.
But these little sands
blowing into my eyes
can't stop me from finding

my way back home to

you. Beauty everywhere,
glamour all around me and
despite all things beautiful,

beside you, none of them
compares.

# Life Is a Song

In my ruins, I danced.

In my reign, I danced.
I take whatever life

throws at me joyfully.

For life is a song, and I
must continue to
learn to dance to its

moody
melodic tunes.

# I Will Rise stronger

Your love compels my heart to beat forever!

# Love Is a Finders Keeper

                                    Many have found me and
tossed me aside, hoping it
would be my loss. But today,
under this diamond sky,
held in your warm embrace,
my face shines. Held in your
magical gaze, I am an
unbreakable glass.
Glinting of glory, I have now become.
Tight like soil holding

                                    the roots of a tree,

I perform a firm dance.
Dancing in many windy rains have
given me this firm stance.
I know what this means,
I will never let go of
this lovely feeling.
It is true, what is deserving
of you awaits you.
It always finds you, once
you've trekked the miles to seek it.
Trust in it, even in your worst
of worries, like I did. I wasn't

                                    looking for you,
                          but you found me. Love.

# I Will Rise stronger

Do you know why you keep getting back up each time you fall in life, my friend? It is because you are a combination of a broken heart and a strong spirit. A mighty warrior!

# I Am Glad I Have You, My Great Friend

Dear great friend, so many moments could have meant nothing without you. Your attention and affection kept me in a forward motion. I am glad I have you, my great friend.

Through my storms, you have been a great calm. Through my dark days, you have been a great lamp, camping with me until the dark skims past. Through our ups and down, we were never on different path. I am glad I have you, my great friend.

In my loneliness, you alone rescued me. In your absence, I sought to find out if you were okay. On slippery grounds, we have heard on one another like solid rocks. I am glad I have you, my great friend.

From class to grass, we have sat and smiled, exchanging a great source of energy and vibe, exchanging compliments about each other's flaws, exchanging feelings and secrets. I am glad I have you, my great friend.

Through boys and men, we have survived. Through jerks and mean guys, we stood up for one another. I am glad I have you, my great friend.

When my shoulders sagged, you have lent me yours and a tissue to sniff into. On phone, we have drained the clock.

It is hard to tell that we aren't from the same tree. For like good apples, we made each other good.

Through the phone, I can hear your sweet smile. Through the rain, you come when I am feeling low, tugging me away from my thorns with your pleasant hugs. You are a true friend forever, and I will never forget that.

Until the day we die, I pray you stay my true friend. You are a true friend forever, and I will never forget that.

# yes I Am stronger than you Think

You gave me hell,
and I gave you kindness
in return. This is how

weak you've
made yourself look. You could
do with this kind of heavenly strength

in your life,
kindness.

# I Will Rise stronger

Love is an artist, and we are its canvas. The best part about love is that it takes our mess and makes it into a beautiful mess!

# Love filler

Your

love took my
melancholy of yesterday

and turned it into

a glory of joy.
And today,
together our souls flow in love,

and our hearts
float with love.

# A Place I Always Wanted

I was looking for the one

place to call home. But
like sieves, conflicted
hands held me, unwilling
to wrap me tight around
their hearts, letting go of
me, draining me away
from themselves.

And now, falling down

all by myself, I fell into
you, unable to continue
my fall, captured by a
determined and decisive
heart. In here, I feel so at
home. You are the one place

I have always wanted.
I stayed.

# Try I Must

Words like knives aimed
at my face, hitting my heart,
leaving me with more than little blood.
A child I was, and now I'm not.

Your words, like the knife, still
bleed me dry. Sad I was, and
silent I was. In pain I was,
and in fear I was. A child
I was, and now I'm not.

But forward I fancy, and
self-love I can. A child I
was, and now I'm not.

Healing I want, and happiness
I need. A child I was, and
now I'm not.

So, try I must, and smile
I must, strong
I must, and forgive I must.
For a child I was, and
now I'm not.

# I Will Rise stronger

Each day gone is a product in our lives. If we don't review them, we will buy into them again tomorrow!

# From Invisible to Indispensable

Invisible I was because I
had nothing to prove.
Not too cool for the fools,
not too smart for the
smart asses. So, behind
closed doors, indispensable I grew.

I buried myself in my books,
never wondering if anything
would check if I was doomed.
Friend and families alike,
no one said hello.
Now I come out a bloom,

everyone wants me in
their rooms.

# Everywhere I Go

Like

a cordless phone,
your love is carried in my
heart to

wherever I go.

I call on your memory

just to hear
your voice.

# I Will Rise stronger

To get your act together, you must first get your facts right. You won't get results until you understand the facts. So ask why!

# A New Mind

Each day, I hide under

my bed, where everything
broken I have kept. But
who am I kidding, hide
and seek isn't my best
trait. My demons know
all my hiding spots all too
well, especially when

my hiding spot is inside

my dark broken mind.
They helped me create
this coping mechanism,
when I needed a place
to silently cry. I need

to move. Today, I must
get me a new mind.

# Little by Little your Life Fades Away

Tick-tock, tick-tock, little
by little your life fades
away. It could be a mile
away, it could be a distance
away. It could be today, it could be tomorrow, but little by
little, your life fades away.
It could be a summer
away, it could be a winter
away. It could be a rain
away, it could be a rainbow
away. It could be a flower
away, it could be a

heartbreak away. It

could be a good night
away, it could be a good
morning away. It could
be a sin away, it could be
a forgiveness away. It
could be a smile away, it
could be one hug away.
Little by little, your life
fades away. It could be a
kiss away, it could be a
sneeze away. Little by
little, your life fades away.
It could be a stretch
away, it could be an itch

away. Little by little, your
life fades away.

# I Will Rise stronger

Love is complex and of many grey areas. But I do enjoy
the simple colours of happiness it has to offer us!

# keep walking the bridge

Determination is the bridge
between intention and destination.
You might not be where you want
                        to be but as long as you keep
going with a determined heart
it won't be long
                                    before you
                                        arrival.

# The difference is you!

You are the difference between
what is and what will be.
For making a difference
starts with you. You can't

make a difference until

you become of essence.
Until your existence provides
a meaningful purpose that
better another's a living experience.

The difference
starts with you!

# Faraway

Every day I looked away

from my problems,
thinking it might get me
far away from them.
But wrong was I for I
couldn't get away from
my problems just by
looking away, just by
taking one step away
from its rotten smell.

I could get away from

my bed, away from my
couch, but away wasn't
far away enough to get
far away from my mind
to think, to be in a different
room where the rotten
smell don't remind me
of its presence. Now that
I have taken more measures,
taken more than one step
every day, I can't smell

this rotten smells again
from this far away.

# This Is My Moment

Could this be the moment where my feet follows my heart?
Could this be the moment where I get better?
Could this be the moment I rise?
Could this be the moment I smile?
Could this be the moment I fly?
Could this be the moment I
start painting colours on my blues?
Could this be the moment I am more gentle and patient
with myself?
Could this be the moment I fall in love?
Could this be the moment I find myself?
If it isn't, I must make it!
For this very sunshine,
this is my moment!

# I Will Rise stronger

Deleted. Text blocked. You are toxic, and I am detoxed of you. Get gone now. Bye now, for good!

# I Am Unbreakable

You

tried to destroy me,
but I am not a toy.

I don't break

in the hands
of men that act like

clumsy
boys.

# I Will Rise Stronger

When God gives you another day of grace, don't
give it away carelessly. Don't exist in it meaninglessly.
Make each moment of it count purposely!

# The Slaves were Brave

The slaves were brave, and their craving was freedom. They waved their shackled palms at the shine of each sunrise. At night time, under the moon, they slaved nonstop, despite their chained ankles.

The slaves were brave. Their patience was never late. They anchored their hope not on violence but on a sage virtue, wisdom. They served with humbleness and reserved their strength to the fateful flight they wanted. Freedom.

The slaves were brave, despite the whips and bruises, the burns under blistered feet, and the wounds around their weakened wrists. They were filled with hope of freedom that they might not even see themselves tomorrow. Still they worked and worked and worked until tomorrow's world of integrated freedom was built.

The slaves were brave, welcoming the notion of inferiority into their nature, stripping themselves bare of all authenticity so the authorities can feel superior. And in discomfort they conformed; in brutality, they conformed; in oppression, they conformed—all so they can free the burden of many unborn generations to come.

The slaves were brave, in spite of the horror and merciless death at the hand of their masters. Through bleeding skin and crushed bones, their hearts still pumped with the hope of God's grace.

The slaves were brave. On pillows made of rocks, they continued to dream soft dreams of happy children, void of the burden of any master's need.

The slaves were brave. On hungry stomachs, the slaves built a home for tomorrow's leaders. When I look at the meritocracy of the world today, I see all colours holding the reigns to success.

The slaves were brave. They took the tales of belief and wonders into our generation, and today, white or of colour, brave is the only colour of success.

# freedom or doom, a man is strong enough to decide

Freedom or doom, a man is
strong enough to decide.
Men, like wood cut from the same
tree we are, even though we become
shaped of different good and gloom.
Men, by axe or saw, a good tree becomes
detached, along side a good heart if
we sway away from good. So let's
carry our hearts like good tools and
put them to good use. For boom,
we all come with good blood from
different roots. But soon, many become
one vessel filled of society's nasty taste.

Men of manhood, proof your good
in your livelihood,
rule your mood with good deeds,
in childhood or in adulthood.
For kings we all
are, even as kids, even with
our many kinks. For
manhood is a beautiful transition
between teenage and the aged,
a fresh flourish we must cherish
because in no time, like fresh fruits
we are doomed to perish.

For like pages in a book, we shall
turn and turn till we reach the last
page of our stage in age. Although
unlike a book, we can't return like a
mere turn to a previously missed page.

Men, take caution of your actions,
for time is forward focused, so let
your deed do more good than wounds.
And when you fail, let your failure
give you wisdom and not unredeemable
regrets, the worst of which is behind
bars for life, for taken another's earned sweat.
For taken another's life for life.

Men, it takes only a second to think.
But if we think that a second is too
long, and we become impulsive and
reckless, until we reach a trigger of ego,
and go to act thoughtlessly just to prove
that we are great at violence,
then a new transition begins to unfold,
where we are uphold with a new
status, monsters. And branded
beneath a man, animals.
So, think before you act,
so your fate and freedom
won't be held by random strangers,
a pen, a hammer and a wig.

Men, if you ever think that a
second is too long to think before
you act, wait till you realise that a
second too late does make a whole
sentence stick a lifetime. And again
if you think that a second is too late
to think before you act, wait till you
are serving a lifetime with at least a
decade longer than the average
estimated mortality.

Men, so guide your years, so your
later years will be filled without
many tears.

Men, hold unto your dream with
your heart, not your sight, nor
your hand nor your ears or
reroute and reboot we shall
become from what we
really want to tell the universe
that we are, if you don't.

Men, when we empty our one
life so others can be filled with a
better living than us, we become
part of the problem, and we beat
ourselves daily until we become
shallow and swollen with hurts.
Until we become like beeping robots,

bleeding from greed of another's need.
But a man who takes charge of his
dream can't be discharged into the
needy greed of another's dream.

Men, Don't let anger linger after
the noon sun gives way to the moonlight,
for the forenoon will suffer a wasteful
mood of a day's bloom.

Men, if we play foul in life against
our neighbour just to be cool, alone
like a crook in a coop we will become,
after we've stooped to society's fools.

Men, pour love into your soul and let
the door off the wall that hides your
fears and scars so that the one you love
won't hurt because you hurt them
when you are hurt.

Men, eat the grape that's yours,
so your grave will bloom with
fresh colourful flower given by the
one that loved you dearest after the
changing seasons of nature takes turns.
For freedom or doom, a man
is strong enough to decide.

I Will Rise stronger

To Settle For Less Is a Reckless Rest!

# Hell and Holy Grail

Your love gave

me so much
insight into all my
oversights
from the past. For
even though
I now find myself in
a heaven
of love, through hell
I have come,

and tough demons

I have conquered.
After much patience,
your love
welcomes and endures.
And now,
through your love, my
soul dines
among angels. My
heart now dwells

in a heaven filled from
holy grail.

# I Am My Own Mountain

Looking

back, from this
height where I can now
sight light, from this might
where I feel just right,

everyone posing as an

obstacle were made of tiny
stones. For the mountain
once in front of me were

not of anyone
but of myself.

# Guided By Faith

When the heart speaks,

quiet your hands and listen
with your feet boldly.
For everything

drawn away

from you is meant to create
space for everything daring
you on. Let faith take you

to a better
fate.

# My Age Has Come Calling

Gone were the days of strength and time. But a cow with healthy limbs, a sound mind and a bucket I still have. The milk is out, and I was no good with my youth. I have wasted all the milk in haste to please. I have almost killed the cow in haste to pleasure. But now,

I am older, and I have nothing to show for my age. Now I go back to where I should have started from all along, seeking guidance from the one who created me in his own image. And so I say, guide my ways, tell me when, slow me down, show me how, lead me there, pour me more grace.

These words I peruse
daily with the one above.
I don't want to steal my
own life away from me

before I have nothing
left of it. My age has called.

# I Will Rise stronger

The ruins I met yesterday pointed me in
the direction of joy I am at today!

# Fight the Fight Right

For a long while, I have
ignored the elephant in
the room, not wanting
to fight the triumphant
fight to win against it.
Among decayed apples,

I have chosen to lie,

blending right in where
opportunity might mistake
me. Betraying myself
of everything I deserved.
Now I have chosen to
hold my intentions, not
with a slack commitment,
for my misery holds me

with a firm grip. Today
I must fight the fight right.

# Ignored My Distractions

As soon as I opened my eyes, my phone summon's me to itself with a little blinking light. This means juicy updates from friends and strangers, but I have things to do today.
I know that once I swipe I would slide away from my intention. So ignored I left my addiction. So, before I do something

that I might regret

before I fall asleep again, I reframed from my distraction. I must get disciplined with my mind if I really want this positive change. Distractions not today, not tomorrow, and am sure not the days after that shall I choose you first over my intentions to do the right things to make myself better. I must keep ignoring

my distraction to get to my intended destination.

# I Will Rise stronger

My soul feels held in a safe heart seeing
you treat others with kindness!

# The One Made For Me

On this earth, my ears
have heard about heavens
from men with hot smooth
tongues. On this earth, my
heart has seen so much
hell from hot rough hands.
Love to them were tales they
never took seriously. But
when I see you, I believed
in love again, for I see no
deceit in every word you

speak. For your lips carry

great promises of blooms not
like those goons. And I know
a goon when I see one, they
have taught me every trick in
their dirty books. And I know
that they don't make men like
them in heaven where you
came from. And knowing
what you are through your
actions so far, I know you
were made from heaven to
take me through a heavenly
journey back with you. For

you are the one I have been
praying for.

# I love it here right next to you

I love it here right next to you,
on your chest, with my
arms around your torso.
I love it here next to you
with my gaze on your
peaceful face, watching
you while you sleep, while
you dream of the magic
you've heard about me.
Like a book, I satisfied you.

Last night, like chapters.

I turned to your every touch.
All these years, you never
put me back on the shelve
of shame, among the dust
and the abandoned, like
others had. I will always
be right here when you
open your eyes again,
when you pick me up again,
when you spend this raining
day indoor learning
everything about me.

I love it here, right next to you.

# Bold Prayers of Faith

                         I have
bills and debt high
up to my neck, but this trek
won't be the end of me. For
                  I will work hard and hard and
hard till I see them no more.
God give me more gracious
days so I can make it right.
Amen to this, then up on my
                   heels I head out and hustle
                            hard again.

# Pride

There is nothing wrong to be
proud with who you are for
we can't live life right until we
take pride of the life in it.
So pride I take in everything I produce:
For my sake, I spark with pride.

In my smile, I take pride.

In my tears, I own pride.
In my mistakes, I reflect with pride.
In my brilliance, I share with pride.
In my job, I work with pride.
In my judgement, I act with pride.
In my wins, I cheer with pride.

For I am proud of everything
that's come out of me.

# words of wise windows

I spent many days dimmed
even when I had so much light
within me. But tonight, while
I lie, all alone, the windows
tells me something: The moon,
                    even alone, shines bright. And
today, like my wise window,
I have this to tell you: Even
alone, we must be ourselves,
we must shine bright like our
                    nature has created us
                    to be.

# I Will Rise stronger

Don't get me wrong, I love waking up and staying in bed all day. But I love making my bed comfortable enough, so when I lay back down in it, I don't have to worry about the problems tomorrow morning on my days off!

# confident faith

The

weight of troubles
never troubled me,

overcomes me
with strength, unmatchable

for my faith

by any
demise.

## I won't stop

A

breath, a minute, a day,
a week, a month, a year,

no matter

how hard I must
work, no matter how long
I have to wait, I won't stop
until I see my

dream
come true.

## Deal With It

I
am different now, I won't
shrink just because you
prefer the lesser version

of me and the weaker version
of me. I have dealt with me
according to the version of

greatness I need to be.
Live with it.

# This Is Me Now

You can't force the shoes
from years ago onto my
feet today. For I have overgrown
your memory of me. I will never
settle for who others are use to.

For my new wings calls upon
me to stop being the child who
I was known by and start being
the adult who I have grown up
to know.

This is all you have
of me. This is me now.

# I WiLL RiSE stronger

If you stand in your way, you won't be able to move forward. If you are still where you wished you weren't before, you've been standing in your way all along!

# on-route to Healing

The

scars on my skin
remind me that I am

made to heal when I hurt

again. And with a smile, I
endure this pain. With hopefulness,
I see these wounds on

their way to<br/>healing again.

# BELIEVE

Believe

in the magic
within you. There
is more in you to come.

For your soul,

like the sky,
has more

than darkness
to give.

# At This Phase

                          I am at this wonderful phase
where my face shines,
where my toes curl with
pleasure, where my curves
move with cuteness, where
my heart hums with happiness.
                    When I look at my own reflection
through the mirrors that once
shared my shattered tears and
sadness with me in my darkest
lonely moments. I see that I am
indeed strong! I am indeed
                          a warrior. My own glow
                          applauds me now!

## Better Off Without You

You ask me how I am still
standing with my head raised
high? It's this: I was good
before I met you, but your

worst brought out the best

in me. You taught me hurt.
I taught me healing. I am
better off without your kind.
You were a great reminder,

of how strong
I really am.

# Never Ever Again

My

goodbye is forever.
I mean it hurts

to remember

all the hurt, but
it reminds me
never to fall for

you
again.

# I Will Rise stronger

To do better, you must first do your best!

# I can Feel the Good News

Like a cocooned caterpillar
turned into a butterfly, I
can see the crack of good news.
I can feel the hope of good news
as if physically held inside
my palms. Like rainbow after
a rain, I can feel it in my bones.
Like sunshine after a sunset,
I can feel it in my veins.
Like flowers once planted as
seeds beneath the soil, I can

feel it in my soul.

Like a landing plane after a
long flight, I can feel it in my faith.
Like a sailor reaching a harbour.
I can feel it in my heart.
Like the skilled roar of a lion,
I can feel it in my voice.
Like February after January,
I can feel it in my steps.
Like the ticking down of an
explosive, I can feel it on the
counting of my fingers.
I can feel it in my very being

that good news will
come very soon.

# Thank you poems

This daily, dominating smile
on my face was once
diminished in my heart
by pain of my past. And this pain
is like a disease to my heart.
And I have felt rage, and
I have felt hate. I was left
a wreckage. I was delivered
like a destroyed package
to my mind. But now, I often
put my feet up, hold a nice
drink to my lips while the air around
me fills with a soulful melody.
I get lost in a few great poems to find
peace within my soul,
and I find love growing like
trees after each page read.
Each word opens
the closet to my soul and
pours honest emotions into it.
And each time my heart heals
as it becomes less of its
illness, I realised that rage is the
symptoms of hate, and that
love is the cure for hate.
I have found love in self-care,
in self-confidence, in self-love,
in self significance.

# Act of Love

You paint a view.

I build a wall. You bring
the nails. I bring the hammer.
I anchored you to my heart.
You honored me with your soul.
You give me. I gift you.
This is what the act of love
is all about—my paper heart.
In someone else's story,
we are merely pens destined
to be drained, emptied,

and chucked away.

But you weren't just
anyone. You were my one.
So blank and inkable you are.
So frank and loveable you are.
For you, I gladly inked
myself empty, filling your
heart with the space of me,
with the face of peace.
For you, I gladly inked
myself bare, for your
heart wrote passionately
about me. Now, peaceful

in your heart, I will never
fade away. You are my paper heart.

115

## Life People

Life can become.

People can become.
Life is a pen.
Some people are books,
some are authors.
Life can be used,
people can be used.
Among these two

people though, one

writes over what is to
be, the other one gets
written into what to be.
For what will be is based
on who we think we are.

For who we are makes
what will be be.

# Awake

For many years, I was sleeping on my dreams. I was up but not awake. Extinct from success. Discomfort in my mind. Existing but not evolving.

I was frustrated with this exhaustion. I found myself sleepliving. But life made me so bitter that I wanted to taste something better for a change. Addicted and dedicated I became, committed and consistent I became, pursuing my dream with

effort. Change I taste now, great it tastes now.

# I Will Rise stronger

When you have a dream, never question your ability to achieve it. Question the negativity that says otherwise!

# They will come around Better

As a visionary who want to evolve, I must remind myself that we must be fully dedicated with our intentions in order to achieve our goals. Unlike the challenges of self doubt, fear, and lack of resources we might face, the people we love will become among the obstacles that we must overcome on our path to success. The moment I stated that I wanted to fight for what I love, that was the moment the people I loved began to fight against what I love. At first, I didn't get the why behind the grudge, but later on understood that is was part of the sacrifice I must overcome. This is simply because when we decide to make a move, to stand out, people around us are going to scrutinise our new sense of self-belief because they don't understand why we feel like we are something else than what they are. And at first, they won't see us more than what they know us to be. So they might start by questioning our vision, our integrity, our past mistakes. Then they will follow it by questioning our actions. But despite the criticism, despite the lack of support, despite the spite and hate, we must keep focus on our goals. They will come around at some point or another with a better belief of us.

# Fame, Tamed by Peace

I met a stranger today who looks like a beautiful sunrise. She smelled of fame, she looked like a dame but without a name, without a need. She smiled at strangers, she gave to the poor, she helped the aged. She asked me why I do what I do. "I love art," I said. "That's why I draw, that's why I do what I do. It brings peace to my soul like no other." She smiled at me like she did all those strangers. "Peace is an act of freedom," she said, "not reducing oneself to thinking what others might say. Doing what you want to do brings you a sense of control, of freedom, right?" She asked me with her famous smile. I asked her why she does what she does, and here's what she said. "Didn't you get the hint?" she said smiling again. "Now I know I am no saint, I have so many dents of my own, a closet full of bones to pick with myself, but my act wears kindness with decency, for peace is an act of freedom, for peace is what real fame should be about. For unlike fame, peace is uncommon, peace is priceless. And it is like gold in the land of the rich and famous, hard to find in our enriched soil of glory." But out here, in your world, in this world of grace and burden, of men and women, of children and the aged, true freedom blooms. Now on my canvas, she is made of colours of my freedom, and her soul is an art painted in my heart. I will never not know freedom again, I am at peace, priceless.

# I Will Rise stronger

What makes us winners is our awareness of choice. For we can only give ourselves a chance where we believe there is a choice to!

# The real deal is I

My scars hang on my

mind like gold medals
on a wall. Reminding me
that I have been an active

partaker in life, that I

am a real contender in
life, and that all these

battles I faced and fought
it made me a real champion.

# Hanging on

No one sees the war behind
my eyes, for I wear courage
like make up. But when the
night calls, I can't brush them
off under the carpet. But I know
that I am not alone in this war.
And this gives me hope that we
are all hanging on to life the
best we humanly possibly can.

# Expect it, but respect you

When you respect yourself
enough nothing unexpected
will dim your light. The truth is,
some will misunderstand you,
some will hate on you, some
will be unpleased with you,
some will backstab you,
some will call you crazy,
but none of them has the
power to put off the passion
burning within you except
you. Expect it all, but respect
you among all.

## I Got Me

I stood up for myself once,
and I got this. Who do you
think you are? It was the
best complement anyone

would have given me.

It told me I had redefined myself
into a version of me that
once bowed to the blows

of people who thought
too low of me.

# I Am Impenetrable

Like the weight of a thousand
cinderblocks, the past held my
heart beneath the sea of hope,
trying to rot my chains of hold,
trying to keep me from seeing
any shine in the sky. But I am
as solid as they come, an
indestructible being. My soul
is an impenetrable volt filled
with an indestructible gold.

# I Will Rise stronger

To achieve your intention, your action has to be compatible with your interpretation of yourself!

# A Bird's Nature to Fly

All my life,

they have tried
to push me down, but they
never learned.

It's a bird's

nature to fly. Upward I rise
again, higher

I fly
again.

# No stranger

I
am no stranger to pain,
I am no stranger

to sorrow,

but I keep surviving,
for I am know

of joyful
melody.

# A Persistent seed

I

never thought I was
capable of growth until I

meet a sunny sky. I couldn't

see through the dark, but
I got through the night. All

because I craved to see
what's above the soil.

# I Will Rise stronger

I am not for sale, but you deserve what's priceless. That's why I am all yours!

# RESILIENT SOUL

Despite

life's burden, my
thorns softens as

I toughen,

and through my blues,

I
bloomed.

## caring soul

This always hurts me.

The fact that
I can't heal everyone in

Who's hurt. But I vow to make
everyone I meet feel healed,
with my smile, with my hugs,
with my kindness, with my
compliments,
with my attention,

this world

even if it just for
a minute or so.

# unfazed

My

fears never scare
me, for I have

let them free, for the forest is
never scared of

its
beast.

# A Giving Heart

I have given so much love,
and I have received so little back.
Buts it's okay. For everyone
who have received from me

needed love far more than

my desire to stay whole.
But this feeling, this feeling of
being able to help others
become more than less of

themselves makes my
heart feel whole.

# I Will Rise stronger

Happiness has no business with haste
but trades places with patience!

# strong me

Beneath my skin, I feel the arms of courage. For my scars, my cracks, my flaws,

all of them cured me from my weakness. And now, I release myself into greatness, for in my heart I am

armed
with hope.

# I Belong Here

          I am right where I wanted
to be. For I forgave my
feathers that failed me
when the wind was too

          strong. Through the storms,
my wings stayed well. That's
why I am now where I failed
to be before. For right here is

                just right
to belong.

# Rules of My Heart

                                                Steal

my heart away. I have
left the door unlock.

                                                Steal

my heart away but don't give it
away. These are the terms

                                        to love
                                        me by.

# I Will Rise stronger

Calm in your palm, gentle gaze holding mine. It's nice to be back home again after seeing so many strange faces!

# Lover's Act

There is nothing better than
being consumed by the
breath with which the word's
flow from your parted lips,

when you say the words
I love you. But how lovely
you truly are

consumes
me whole.

# I want to be okay, okay

For

a long time, I was okay
with what's not okay with

me. But now that I know

I deserve more, I won't rest
until I get everything I

want right,
okay!

## Not worth a Drop of me

I

shed these tears not
because of you

but for me.

I should never have given
you my heart. You were never

worth even a
tiny drop of me.

## At Peace With My Pieces

Today,

holding all my
pieces together

is all I

can right now,
and I am

at peace with
that.

# forward focused

I

am so lost in my own self
discovery that it

is impossible

for you to pull me back to
where you found

me easier
to hurt.

# New choice chosenme

I am sorry but not sorry.

Now, this is what we have
become, nothing. For
everything isn't about you no

more. Everything I do now is
for me. For so long, I have
chosen you over me, I have
chosen you before me, I have
chosen you instead of me.

And now I am choosing
me without you.

# What a Shame It Would Be

You owe it to yourself to
become. To enjoy the beauty
of life. It would be a shame
to blame the words of unworthy

being incapable of loving
themselves when God has
granted you a life with love

so you can explore all the
glories in your own lifetime.

# I Will Rise stronger

All I have been is kind to you. But, unfortunately, all you have been is unkind to me. Someday you will come looking for me and I will be there, but not for you!

# Love Myself

From
sunrise to sunset,
from AM to PM, I will

continue to love myself.

For the sky that holds
the rain and clears

the sky for me,
does too.

# Believe in Your Heart

I use to wonder how
long left till I can shine
again. But nature reveals
to me that the sun never
wonders how long till the

darkness will last. The

sun believes in the sky
that holds all things. So,
believe in your heart
that holds all things.
Your time will dawn

again once the purpose
of the dusk is done.

# I Define Me

You act surprised when

I don't cower anymore
under the weight of
your spite. "Nice to meet
you," says the new strong

me! I am defined by me,

not by the mean you.
I might have no control
over your words describing
me. But my own actions,

that is the dictionary
that defines me.

# quiet please critics, says my loud smile

When they thought I
wasn't carved by the
God who made all things
great, God stepped in
and shined me with a
new light of purpose.
Giving me the go ahead
to go ahead. He will be
with me through it all
he promised. I won't
let him down I promised.
He will help me from
heaven, he promised.
I will release me from
my own hell I promised.
I filled my ears with prayers.
I walked with purpose.
I wore blisters like shoes.
I wore callouses like gloves.
I endured the discomfort
with courage, knowing that
it would all pay off soon
enough. I can smile
proudly now because
my work ethic silenced
all negative critics. So,
quiet please critics,
says my loud smile.

# Be Intent with Your Day

Don't
let a day go by
without having a conscious
experience of it.

For each day
we wake can be the last of
everything our

heart wanted
to do to be happier.

# JUST BE

Be

passionate about what
excites you.

about what lights your

Be excited

soul

anew.

# Rebuilding Me Again

My
life seems to be everywhere,
but I am handling it, putting me
first so I can put things in order.
I am gonna heal from this heap
of mess. And don't get me wrong,
I am not in denial that I am apart,
but I am a rebuildable puzzle and
not shattered pieces. And as I
figure life out slowly,

I will put
me together again.

# I Will Rise stronger

*Put your talent out there, follow it with a visible commitment, and let everyone important know that you are the real deal-breaker. Let them know that you are worth a shot!*

# Dream Makers

Dream makers are doers.
Hold onto to your dream. Go
for your dream while you still
can. Don't clown around all
your life. Wrap your heart
around your dreams. Wrap
your hands around your dreams.
Lead your feet towards it until
you make it happen. For when
the grave finally holds your
bones and soul, it crushes
your dreams alongside your

body. And everything you
craved and wanted, but never
made, will laugh at you silly.
Jokes on you, sucker, they
would say alongside your haters.
Ha ha ha, they would chant
relentlessly for years even while
your body and soul sleeps in
peace but unrest. Dream
makers are doers, but not

while they are dead bones
and souls.

# My Actions Over Your Words

You
trusted me with your
words when you told me I

shouldn't follow my dream,

but I was never good with
keeping words that aren't

mine, and that will never
changed about me.

# This Mess

This
mess hurt less when
I put me first for a change.
And I love it. I will do it over
and and over again if it means
I won't feel this

hurt much
ever again.

# I Will Rise stronger

The best triumph in life is having someone love you more than you know you deserve!

# still in Love With you

I thought I can stop loving you. But you can't stop loving someone just because they said they aren't ready to love. Once again, we meet on the street like two strangers waiting for bus 69, but my heart knows this familiar body like a blueprint of a secret pathway memorised.

But it's your smile that gets my heart going bananas. Your smile is like a favourite music to my heart. My heart beats differently around the glint of your teeth. I will ride it out again till I am distant from you again, my familiar stranger. I hope to see you soon again, I am still in love with you.

# Tired of Being Tired

Before

the sunrise is
fully in display, I am
drained of energy. By

night time, I am fully

empty. This is a life I
must abstain from
continuing. For I was

not placed on this earth
to be drained by life.

# My Anchors

Hope
keeps me beneath
the soil. Faith gets me

above the soil. In-between
beneath and above three
things get me through—self-love, persistence,
and resilience.

# I Will Rise stronger

*I am the moon to my darkness, the sunshine to my day. I am everything I need to sparkle in my life!*

# Holding Hope Firm

At the peak of my

wintery sky, my tears
feel like leaves attached
to branches, falling
without second thoughts

as to whether I am

ready to be bare, exposed,
and vulnerable. But my
heart stands firm in the
root of God's grace, holding
my hope of another

colourful season soon
to come.

# Goodbye Weak Me

Good

for me, be like me,
you can. I stopped

coming back to the

drugs because I said
goodbye to the part of

me that was weak and
wicked.

# Born a Bloomer

I
am created with so
much room to bloom

within me. No matter

how much hate you
empty in my ears.

The love of me continues
to bloom within my heart.

# Un-Dimmable Shine

You can't slaughter

my happiness like a
weak lamb with your

       endless negativity.

Your mood can't glom
my vibe. I glow in any
corner or against any
wall. I am more than

       a lamp. I am a sky of
         sunshine.

# Heart Desires

Nothing

means more

to me than

what my
heart desires.

A happier
me.

# I Will Rise stronger

My dress falls off, and my glory unfolds, beholding your grace. And each time you hold my curves, my body becomes like strings. Each time you touch my body, my heart plays another lively tune, pleasure!

# Till You Are Here

The memory of every
moment with you became
a footprint back to my

happiest moneys in life.

Whenever you are not
here, I have a stroll down
there, just to be with you.
This way

I will be with you till you
are are here.

# Letter of conviction

Dear sadness,

Stop being a clown. I
take myself serious!

Bye, Felicia, hit the road,

shove off, whatever
gets you gone for good.

Sincere,
Me

# My Turn of change

I
closed the window
that holds your view.
I opened the doors that
unfolds my freedom.

It is time for a better
change.

# Irreplaceable. Me

You can replace the

space of me, but you
can't replace my absence,
presence, or my essence.
I am one of a kind. You
should have known that.
And now you are on your
knees, begging me for a

second chance? No kidding.

My heels don't want your
heart moving forward.
The moment you left me
for another, you made me
a second choice. But you
should have known. I am
the only choice for me,
and now, I choose what

you should have chosen
as a first choice, me. Bye.

# A Mess but Fear Less

I am a mess. I am not

fearless. But each time
I take a progressive step
into the unknown, I fear
less and less of the mess

I find myself in. For I am

beginning to understand
that my heart wants what's
best for my soul, and I
can only find it through

the tough unknown path
of self-discovery.

# I Will Rise stronger

You can't put this much effort into surviving
life to this point and then settle for sadness!

# I can, I Am

I can be flawed, but I am awesome.
I can be hurting, but I am healing.
I can be lonely, but I am my best company.
I can be happy, but I am a mess.
I can be a pain, but I am precious.
I can be reckless, but I am sensible.

I can be a goodbye breakup, but I am a hello, wow.
I can be full of darkness, but I am a sky of many colours.
I can be a problem, but I am a remedy.
I can be fragile but I am indestructible.
I can be snail-like, but I am agile.
I can be a flower, but I am the soil.
I can be in love with you, but I am in love with me.

It's okay to be both, I permit myself to be both.

# Feelings of Comfort in Discomfort

I

know that life is very
discomforting, but my

effort and positive results

continue to give me hope
that tomorrow will be
more comforting. This

feeling gives me great
comfort.

# I Will Rise stronger

My heart alone is not enough to love you, I
will love you with my soul, body, and mind,
for as long as I continue to exist. For us!

# Lovers mirror

I
love feeling beautiful
things but to see them
with my eyes is beyond
magical. This is the effect
of your smile. Your smile is
like a mirror, and I can see my
heart smiling at me.

# pain|gain

     Yes, even though my mind dances
with joy, and the bells of my eyes
are ringing with a fierce force of determination,
I won't lie to you now, in my progress,
truth is what I can offer you.
       I am consumed with telling a
story after this storm I know
won't defeat my best. My body
and bones feel this pain,
My soul and heart feel these pains
but my brain that sees the
gain is what chains me to

         this reigns of courage to
          continue to persevere.

# your loss, loser

I
gave you the very
best part of me that
was more than good,
and you couldn't do

good with it: your loss,
loser!

## It hurts so much

                It hurts so much.

I am full of pain because
I mattered to me.
Because I blame myself
               for giving someone like you,
someone so so so weak,
a chance to get me wrong again.
I deserved better than you,
         I always have. That's why it hurts so much.

# Done with your lame games

For a while now,
you've blamed me
for your mistakes,
unashamed to withhold
blames for your deeds.
And when I confront you,
you play games, threatening

me you would leave me for

another. But, you cannot
tame me anymore with your
games or your lame claims
of promises. I am more
than the flicker of any candlelight.
I am a firestorm burning
with fierce flame. I would
last without your presence.

I can withstand
the absence of you.

# A special kind

                         This

time when you are
ready to love me again,
I will be gone already.

                   I am not a when I am

bored kinda girl. I am

                a now or never kinda
                      woman.

# Live intently

We
can't have happiness
until we live each day

with a sense of intent

until we fill that intent
with purpose. Until we

genuinely live of purpose
purposely.

# I Will Rise stronger

Don't let your pace stop you from finishing. Yes, it hasn't happened yet, but a tortoise never gives up on its journey just because it can't move like a lion or fly like a bird. So go at your own pace. But never stop going until you get home successfully!

# seeds turn trees

Shut the whispery sneers
of sorrow, the mockery
fear of tomorrow, for hope
beats in every heart.
Bit by bit, inch by inch,
dusk through dawn,
we amount to more when
we take the chance to grow:

the sunlight, the raindrops,
the darkness, all here for
us to own. For every mighty
tree started as tiny
seed under similar conditions.
Now they are up to their throne.
So, like seeds turn trees,

we can also become more
than we are known.

# This light you see

"OMG," you say! "Wow, look
at you," you say! "So you are
very famous now," you say!
But what it is, is more
than what you see. There is
more to me than the all
you know. There is more
of me than the less you've
found. This light you see
is a result of many fortresses.

This light you see is a
result of many loneliness.
This light you see has been
the result of much darkness.
This light you see has been
the result after much sadness.
This light you see has seen
so many cloudy skies.
This light you see has
seen so much bitterness,

but this light you see is
only the beginning of my greatness.

# Giving us a chance to try

I won't let go just yet.

Our history hasn't been
all rains and canes. Our
hearts has seen great
times together. So, I will
give us the option to work

on what's not working

because we deserve to
try at least. But, I won't
force you to stay. And if
you've made up in your
heart to leave,
please leave and never

come back. And stay gone,
for good.

# I Will Rise stronger

Your hands feel welcoming, your heart feels like home!

# DarkGlow

I

look at the

bright stars

and they
remind me of

your natural
glow.

# meyouforever

When

your wrinkles are

strong and

your ankles
are weak,

I will still
love you.

# Forgive yourself

You
will never forgive

yourself for yesterday's
mistakes if you partake I
n the entertainment

of self-blame
every other day.

# you've Been strong all Along

About you, they were
wrong for so long.

Look

back into your history,
and you shall see how

strong you've survived
all along.

# Let them go

I made you my everything.

I gave you everything.
More than me, I made
everything about you to
keep you happy, draining

every last smile within

me, so you can be filled
with everything that keeps
a person you love. And still,
you treat me less than
a tiny piece of a whole cake.
Now, I choose to let you go.

The season of us has
finally seized.

# Flaw Flawless Lovers

We

were not perfect,
but we were effective

with our flaws.

That's why we
loved

each other
flawlessly.

## consistent lover

On the 1ˢᵗ of January,
I asked, what do you love

the most about me?
On the 31ˢᵗ of December, with flowers
in my hand and a smile on my lips,

I am still listening
to your answer.

# I feel it too

Whoever

said Love is
real must

have felt all

the butterflies
I am feeling

right now
for you.

# Acceptance

I

love you because

you never tried

to change me.
Instead,

you
appreciate me.

# I am like an ocean

I am like an ocean,

you can't drain me.
I am like an ocean
you can't defeat me.
I am like an ocean you
can't burn me down.
I am like an ocean
you can't kill me.

I am like an ocean,

you can't scoop me dry.
I am like an ocean you
can't move me. I am like an
ocean you can't consume
me. I am like an ocean
you can't control me.
I am like an ocean there
is nothing you can do to hurt me.

I am like an ocean you
have no choice but to live with it.

# open up

Let your fears fall on good
ears. Let your tears fall
on caring faces.
Let their good hearts
feel it. Let it be known
by caring souls. For you
can't bury all of these tiny
hurt inside of you, hoping
that they would die and
fall away like dead leaves

off its branches. You can't
plant all of this little hurt
inside of you, expecting that
they would dry out like
flesh on bones buried
inside a coffin, consumed
by six feet of dirt beneath the earth.
Instead, the hurts will rise like phoenixes,
creating a flux within your
heart and worsen everything
fixed about you. They will taunt
you like an army of ants, and
in their tinny minor forms,
they will emerge and merge

into an invisible hand,
edging you to every tiny insecurity.

# when a man be. he stops becoming

When a man be, he stops becoming. So, society, what do we believe our men can only do? Be? Limited, lessened, labeled as a cheap price tag? And hung on a macho dogma? We've sold men short for centuries to babies new to our cities. Those kids who are now part of our familiar towns have become nothing more than what we've sold: limited, lessened, violent, emotionless. We've labeled them as worthless males because we've only taught them to be a man and nothing more.

So, when will we encourage men to become happier, loving, and better versions of themselves? Is, be a man really what makes a man today? or is it our fantasy of what we want to make of a man, contrary to what men are born to become? More than minimal. "Be a man!" Society says. "Be a boy!" Society says. "Be strong, be misogyny," they add. But before we became anything we are now known to be, we were merely sperm and eggs. Before now, men were tasteless of careless violence, tasteless of helpless macho, tasteless of senseless ego.

Before we became masculine, we were all parts of a feminine foetus. Before we became bros, we were all embryos, like what females were before they became women, sperm and egg we all were. It was how we all started.

Before the muscle and bone mass, we were all sperm and egg.

Before the testicles and testosterone, we were all sperm and egg.

Before society's definition of masculinity and it's conformity, we were all sperm and eggs.

Like fragile fluid, we were, capable of transformation, qualified to become. But look at us now, loveless of ourselves, loveless of our kind. Hateful of our genes, shameful of our emotions. We are held back by a society filled with a false sense of what makes being a man that we are restricted from becoming more than the concept of a strong, violent, emotionless man? "Don't be such a girl. Men don't cry!" Society says. But why did God give men tears if not to shed them when in need? Do men bleed? Yes. Do men die, yes? So we aren't immortal after all. Even Jesus wept. A God who understands what it means to be hurt, to be human, to be a man or a woman.

Why did God create women? If not to help men see that they can't make the world better by being misogyny? Isn't it all because women are a prime example that a man can become more than be: alone, strong, aggressive, violent, and nothing more? Our society thinks men who express love are weak, and those who don't are real men. But no man is without tears. No man is without emotion. For we were born with tears in our eyes, and we were strong even before we came into this world with our baby cries. From tiny embryos, we became warriors. Our existence emerged from lovemaking, not from strength or aggression; love has always been in our DNA, not hate. As men, we must make loving ourselves a mission so we can love what becomes of us, so we can love the woman who has welcomed us into her heart as if it were this version of us we now love with passion. Let a man be helped become better, not just be.

# I Am on Team Me

My bag of commitment
is all packed.
I won't slack this time.
I promise.
I promise I will have

my own back.

I will crack my own
fortune.
I will cheer me all the
way through it all. I am
on Team Me. I've got to

do this for me. I've got
my own back.

# I Will Rise stronger

Your voice is my favourite song!

# Amplified Lovers

Nothing amplifies love
more than giving yourself
vulnerably to someone

you trust so strongly,

knowing that they
might not be perfect in
their might, but they are

committed to holding you
with all their heart.

# I Will Rise stronger

Love is pure pain. But a great pleasure
if you find it in the right one!

# LoveLifeline

Every time my heart beats,
it tells a magical story
about us and forever.
Your love is
my lifeline.
If my heart ever stops
beating, it is because you
stopped loving me.

I

The end of us does not
mean the end of I.
I was me before us.
I can continue with
me without you.

# I Will Rise stronger

Let where you come from keep you humble, and let where you are going keep you hungry!

# An ugly ride

It is cute that you
call me a beautiful princess.
But please call me a

beautiful progress.

It has been a long ugly
ride to get to this look-good,

feel-good place in my life.
But I am not done just yet.

# Effort and colours

Greener grass,

the
chores of

effort.

I keep
working with

all I've
got.

# It's All Coming Back to Me

They say, when you
give more you receive
more. So, here I am,
giving my self more of
what I have given to

others who have left
me empty. Time, happiness,
self-love, and self-care. I am
finally receiving what I
should have a while

ago. I am now at the
receiving end of me.

# Happiness Awaits your consent

The future is eager to
meet you. The present is
expected to take you there.
But neither will force you

to move forward.

You must decide what you
want for yourself, regret
or a raise above your misery?
You have a free will.

Happiness needs your
consent to help you!

# persistent Try

I couldn't heal through
this fall. The wall is
just damn tall. But
still, I must try another
crawl. Perhaps a cure
await me. Perhaps a

wonderful friend awaits

me. Perhaps a happier
me awaits me. But if I
don't break down these
walls, if I don't get through
the hell, I shall continue
to live with the certainty

that I won't ever leave
this hell.

# I Will Rise stronger

My heart ignites like stars from a distant sky when you are close to me!

# Teach Me Oh Lord

On my knees, I know to ask, Lord.
On my heels, I learn to lean
on your words, lord.
Teach me, Lord, guide me, lord.

I don't know much of what
I am doing, but I know how
to learn. Let's go, Lord, play
the music of grace again

tomorrow, make it rain
again oh Lord.

# Lonely Growth Is worth It

Don't be scared to grow

alone. In my own loneliness,
I learned that every tree

that grew beneath the

soil grew alone until it
could have its own branches
of colours, leaves, and fruits

to share its own
company with.

# I smell perfect Timing

No time is ever going

to be perfect to start
my journey of happiness.

But I am perfectly fine

with starting it this time.
For now smells of a perfect
timing, and I can smell the

hope of me smiling like a<br>true champion.

# I Will Rise stronger

What made you great once made you uncomfortable!

# Pennies in Pocket, Treasures I Mind

I had pennies in my pocket
but treasure in my mind.
The clock is ticking and
my back is edging against
the wall. I gotta keep inking
my thinking. I knew the
next six months would
be brutal, but what lies

ahead if I don't take

matters into my hands
would be far more lethal.
So I worked on my talent,
I work with the latest trend.
I did all this work because
I am worth the sacrifice.
I was tired of the hurt, I
was tired of not having
much. I am born for much
more, I won't be like those
sort, settling for less than
life's lions share. I won't
settle for pennies in my

pocket, when I have treasure
in mind.

## convinced.

Years ago,

I was convincing
myself that I was worth

the fight. Today, look at

me, with my trophy smile,
with my happy face.

I am convinced,
I was worth a shot.

# I Am Certain of Becoming

I

don't know what is
to come,

but I know

what I will become:

stronger, faster, better,
happier.

# I Will Rise stronger

Despite the rain of yesterday, each new day is a song of hope. Glad I am. Dance, I shall. Rejoice, I will!

# you are alive

I know that yesterday
might have felt like hell.
Yesterday, you might
have thought that you
wouldn't survive it, but
here you are, well and
alive because the Lord

isn't ready for you to go.

The Lord has made another
day available to aid you
in your need. Can't you
tell by this unused sky?
Can't you feel this
beautiful sunshine of hope?
Can't you tell? Your heart is

still beating. You are alive,
and that's what matters the most.

1. Until we hatch, we remain like fragile eggs. Until we find our purpose, we remain life's puppet.
2. Once we betray our purpose, all earnings will never be good enough.
3. Think about your finances before you have to worry about them.
4. I had to get lost in order to find myself. It was inevitable.
5. A pure act of kindness is a cure for hopelessness.
6. Do what you can but make sure it was the best you could at this moment in time.
7. To stay motivated, you must have a motive that meets a means.
8. When you prioritise your emergencies, you get more from your effort.
9. Our past has shaped us for so long that we falsely feel like we have no room left to carve ourselves into the new form we want.
10. Hanging onto an old upset cannot help the mindset find peace. Resort we must to moving on in order to reset peace.
11. Misery always smells of lack of purpose in life.
12. To have more in life, we must not be lost in people's list of needs.
13. We can get anywhere in life from anywhere in life.
14. Nobody should need you more than you need yourself.

15. Each time we don't try harder, we miss what could have been. And what we could have been is always better than what is.
16. A few little wise words are better than a heap of nonsense.
17. When greatness is bestowed within you, nothing else will ever be enough to satisfy your discomfort.
18. Sometimes, some things aren't worth the dance. Sometimes, some people aren't worth the rain.
19. How we approach the present determines what we meet in the future.
20. Don't settle only on what you know. Seek more, know more, do more, become more.
21. We all have the power to change our lives, we just have to be decisive about what kind of life we really deserve for ourselves.
22. It is impossible to excel into greatness until we've put aside the fear of being laughed at.
23. Keep your wheels going, keep on your heels, focus on your needs, you will heal soon enough.
24. A great life is a process of many steps and a pattern of a few good habits.
25. Fear is part of existing. But fear is diminished by living.
26. Be nice. Be wise. But most importantly, don't be naive.

# Author's departing note

Many people are comfortable with the discomfort of doing less in life than the discomfort of doing more in life. They think that by doing less, they can preserve the little energy they have left, but in reality, they are merely draining away the energy that is enough to change their circumstances. Thus, they are simply missing out on the everyday possibility of achieving much more in life. This is why my books are so important in life. I want to reveal to my readers that they have enough in their tank of energy to get them out of mediocrity into a superior lifestyle of health, wealth, and happiness. This is why I write!

As a writer I constantly think about the domino effect of success, of leadership, of receiving and giving. I know that I can't inspire the whole world alone, but with every work I ink, I think of inspiring at least just one person who can go on and inspire another, who can go on to inspire another, and so on.

Thank you from the bottom of my heart for getting this copy of my book. I hope that you found something here to help you in your journey of self-discovery.

Printed in Great Britain
by Amazon